Visual Basic.NET All Versions

Visual Basic.NET All Versions

Ali Akbar
Zico Pratama Putra

Kanzul Ilmi Press

2017

First Printing: 2016

Second Printing: 2017

Kanzul Ilmi Press
Woodside Ave.
London, UK

Bookstores and wholesalers: Please contact Kanzul Ilmi Press email

zico.pratama@gmail.com.

Trademark Acknowledgments

Ordering Information: Special discounts are available on quantity purchases by corporations, associations, educators, and others. For details, contact the publisher at the above-listed address.

Contents

CHAPTER 1 INSTALLING AND UNDERSTANDING VISUAL STUDIO'S INTERFACE

Before you can practice the VB.NET programming techniques, first, you have to install the visual studio and then understand the function of many parts of the visual studio workspace. This chapter describes how to install visual studio and then describes the function of many parts of visual studio workspace.

1.1 Development IDE Installation

To make a program, you need an IDE (Integrated development environment). For Visual basic.net, you need an IDE called the Visual studio. Visual studio is not only for visual basic.net, but also for another programming languages created by Microsoft such as visual c#.

VB.NET can only be developed using VS (visual studio). It's different with another programming language such as JAVA that can be developed using multiple IDE, such as Eclipse, Netbeans or Borland-Developed IDEs.

By using a single tool, VB programs developed using Visual Studio.NET will be more integrated and having fewer compatibility issues compared to programming languages that can be developed using more than one tool.

Before you install visual studio, below are system requirements you have to fulfill:

- Windows 7 SP1 (x86 and x64)
- Windows 8 (x86 and x64)
- Windows 8.1 (x86 and x64)
- Windows Server 2008 R2 SP1 (x64)
- Windows Server 2012 (x64)
- Windows Server 2012 R2 (x64)

There are also components you have to prepare before installing Visual Studio:

- IE 10, some components may not work 100% if you don't install IE version 10 or above.

The hardware system requirements are:

- 1.6 GHz Processor or faster.
- 1 GB RAM (1.5 GB if you want to install it on virtual machine)
- 10 GB empty space on your hard disk
- 5400 RPM Hard drive
- A video card that can run DirectX 9 with min resolution 1024 x 768.
- Internet Connection.

Below are steps to install visual studio IDE:

1. Click 2x on Visual Studio.NET installer file to run it, then check on **I agree on license terms and privacy policy**.

Figure 1.1 I agree on License terms and privacy policy

Figure 1.2 Remove option on the second checkbox

2. If you don't want to join VS Experience Improvement Program, remove the second checkbox and click Next. This will reduce your bandwidth consumption.

3. On **Optional features to install**, you can add additional features you want to install.

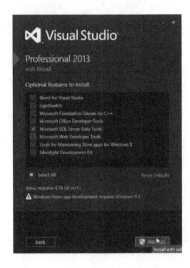

Figure 1.3 Setting addition features to install

4. Click **the Install** button and wait until the installation ends perfectly.

Figure 1.4 Finishing installation

5. If the installation finished, click Launch to run the program.

Figure 1.5 End of installation

6. When the program first time launched, you'll see this interface.

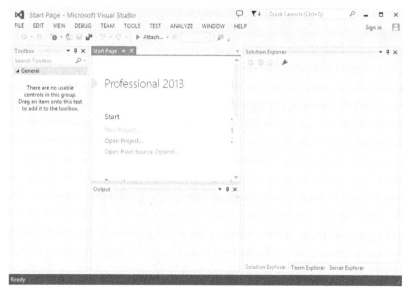

Figure 1.6 Visual Studio IDE first time launched

1.2 Creating First Project

To see the complete interface of VS, you have to make a project first. Here are some steps you can do to make a project:

1. Click **File > New Project**.

Figure 1.7 Menu File > New Project

2. A new window titled **New Project** will emerge.

Figure 1.8 New Project window to create a new project

3. Choose application type "Windows Forms Application", This is the name for regular Windows program. In this example, i will name this project "Halo Dunia". An Indonesian word for "Hello World"

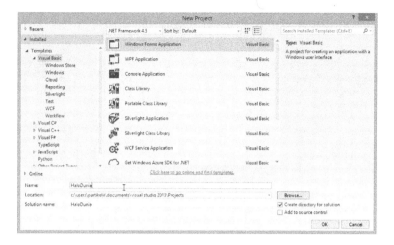

Figure 1.9 Entering program's name

4. When the project opened, all interface's part will suddenly have lots of buttons and panels which you can access to develop a program.

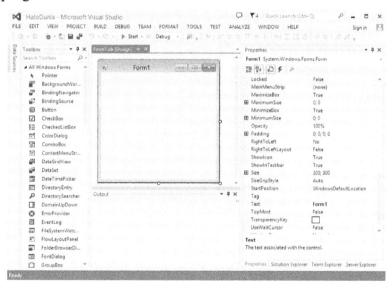

Figure 1.10 Interface of VS.Net while the project opened

1.3 Knowing the IDE Interface's Parts

To show full parts of the IDE's interface, you have to open a project by using these steps:

1. Click on **File > Open Project** menu.

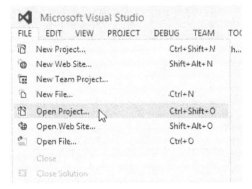

Figure 1.11 File > Open Project Menu to open a project

2. Choose which folder you want to open.

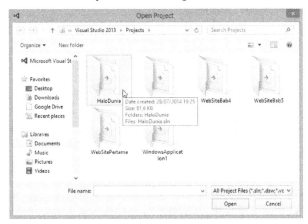

Figure 1.12 Chose project folder to open

3. The project will be opened on a VS window.

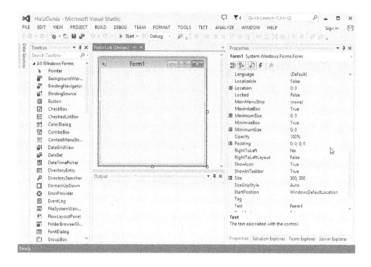

Figure 1.13 Project appeared on VS Window, and default form will be opened

1.3.1 Introducing The Menus

There are many menus in Visual studio, first is File menu. This menu handles project's file operations. Some important menus are:

1. New Project: Create a new project.

2. New Website: Create a new website (eg: using ASP.NET).

3. New Team Project: Create a team based project.

4. New File: Create a new file.

5. Open Project: Open a project.

6. Open Website: Open a website.

7. Open File: Open a new file

8. Add: Add some items to the project file.

9. Close: Close opened project.

10.   Save: Save a project.

11.   Save All: Save all files in the project.

12.   Recent Files: Display MRU (most recently used) files.

13.   Exit: Exit from Visual Studio.

Figure 1.14 File Menu

Edit menu contains menus important to do some editing on the file. Some important menus on this menu are:

1. Undo: Undo the last action done.

2. Redo: Undo the last undo.

3. Cut: Cut values (text, value, number, etc) and then you can paste this cut values using **Paste** button/menu.

4. Copy: Copy values that can be pasted later using **Paste** button/menu.

5. Paste: Display or paste the value from clipboard collected from menu Cut or Copy.

6. Delete: Delete some values.

7. Select All: Choosing all objects.

8. Find and Replace: Find texts and replace it with other texts automatically.

9. Navigate To: Navigate to a certain part of the document.

10. Bookmarks: Bookmark some parts of the document.

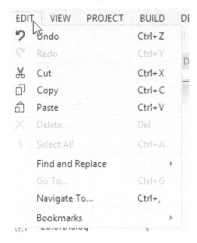

Figure 1.15 Edit menu

View menu used to access and see certain components from Visual Studio. To access and view certain components, you can use these menus:

1. Solution explorer: Open the solution explorer window.

2. Team Explorer: Open the Team Explorer window.

3. Server Explorer: Open the Server Explorer window to see activities on the server.

4. Bookmark Window: Open the bookmark window.

5. Call Hierarchy: Open call hierarchy window.

6. Class view: Open class window.

7. Object browser: Open Object browser window.

8. Error List: Display errors that exist.

9. Output: Display output window.

10.   Start Page: Display start page.

11.   Toolbox: Display toolbox window

12.   Full screen: Make the visual studio screen become full.

Figure 1.16 View Menu

Project Menu contains some menus to manage some items in the project. Here are some important menus from this menu:

1. Add Windows Form: Add new windows form to the project

2. Add User Control: Add new user control to the form

3. Add Component: Add a new component to the form.

4. Add Module: Add a new module to the project.

5. Add Class: Add a new class to the project.

6. Add New Data Source: Add new data source. You'll need this menu when you create a database project.

7. Add New Item: Add a new item to the project.

8. Add Existing Item: Add new item from existing item.

9. Exclude from the project: Exclude items from the project.

10. Add Reference: Add a reference to the project.

11.   Show All Files: Add all file.

12. Set as Startup Project: Set an item as a startup project.

13. Properties: Display properties from the project.

Figure 1.17 Project menu

Build menu used to build the solutions to become an application. Here are some important menus from Build menu:

1. Build Solution: Build solution's files to become an application.

2. Rebuild solution: Rebuild solution's files to become an application.

3. Clean Solution: Doing clean process on the solution.

4. Build project: To build the project.

5. Configuration Manager: Display Configuration Manager window.

Figure 1.18 Build menu

Debug menu is used to debug and run a program. You can search for errors by using this menu. Below are menus available on Debug menu:

1. Start Debugging: Start doing debugging process while running the program.

2. Start Without Debugging: Start/Run the program without doing debugging.

3. Exceptions: Run exceptions.

4. Performance and Diagnostics: Checking the performance of the program, and doing some diagnose on the programs if a problem arise.

5. Step Into: Step into a certain part of the program.

6. Step Over: Step over a certain part of the program.

7. New Breakpoint: Add breakpoint. You can check some values or logics in this breakpoint. Whether it's true or not? Error or not?

Figure 1.19 Debug menu

Team menu used to Access Team Foundation Server. This will make teamwork programming easier to be performed.

Figure 1.20 Connect to Team Foundation server

Tools menu contains some tools that can be used to ease the programming activities. Some menus on Tools menu are:

1. **Attach To Process**: Doing some attachment to some process.

2. **Connect to database**: Connect the database as a data source.

3. **Connect to Server**: Connect to a server, you need to do this if you want to connect to the database.

4. **Add in Manager**: Add-in Manager.

5. **Extensions and Updates**: See the extensions' list and update the extensions if latest version available.

6. **Options**: Manage options from various aspect of the visual studio.

Figure 1.21 Menu Tools di Visual studio

Test menu is used to test the program. there are several menus on Test menu:

1. Run: To run the program.

2. Debug: To debug a program.

3. Test settings: Access some test properties.

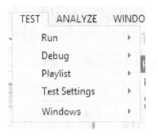

Figure 1.22 Test Menu

Analyze menu, used to analyze various things in the visual studio. Some menus are:

1. Performance and Diagnostics: To check the performance and to diagnose the error.

2. Profiler: Checking the profile

3. Run Code: Run the code.

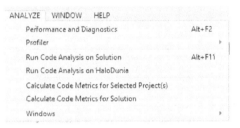

Figure 1.23 Menu Analyze

Window Menu is used to access and manage windows in visual studio. Some important menus here are:

1. New Window: To open a new window.

2. Split window: Split one window into two.

3. Float: Makes window floating.

4. Dock: Makes window docked to a certain area of Visual studio.

5. Auto Hide: Makes window hidden if it's not accessed.

6. Auto Hide All: Makes all windows auto-hide.

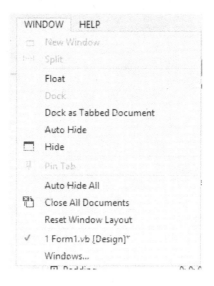

Figure 1.24 Window menu

Help Menu used to show help functions.

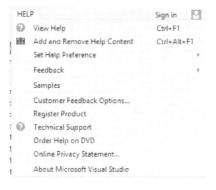

Figure 1.25 Menu Help

1.3.2 Visual Studio Panels

Visual studio also have panels, Every panel has its own function. You can customize this panels, eg: hide the panel you don't need and show the panel you need, etc.

1. **Data sources** are used to display database source used. This is only utilized when you create a program with database.

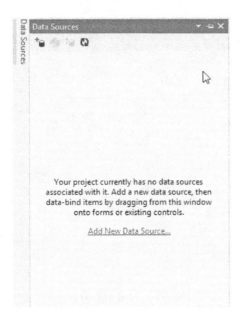

Figure 1.26 Data sources panel

2. **Toolbox**: Contains many components and objects. You can add these components and objects to your program.

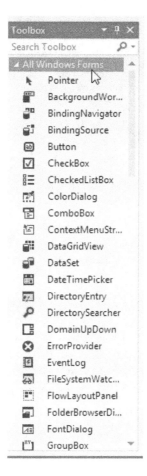

Figure 1.27 Toolbox panel

This toolbox can be categorized. Each tool will be showed below its parent category.

Figure 1.28 Toolbox categories

3. Working area: This is the central panel, where the form of your raw program displayed. If you double click on the form or above objects, a code window will be displayed. This is the code you write to control the object behavior if the object is clicked.

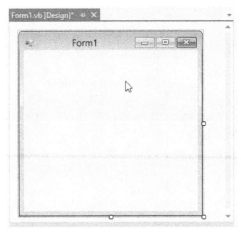

Figure 1.29 working area panel

4. Output: Output panel display output messages released by the program. it makes programmer's task easier while executes and debugs the program.

Figure 1.30 Output panel

5. Properties: Display several object's properties.

Figure 1.31 Properties panel, display properties value of an object

6. **Solution Explorer**, display components of the opened solution.

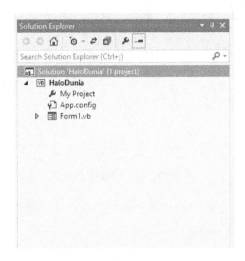

Figure 1.32 Solution explorer

7. Team Explorer: Display users connected to the team.

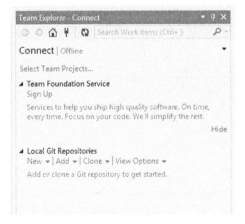

Figure 1.33 Team Explorer

8. Server Explorer: display objects on the server.

Figure 1.34 Server Explorer

1.4 Net Framework

Net Framework is a framework in which all programs build by visual studio dot net run above this framework. So if you want to run the program on other operating systems that haven't had this framework (for example the good old days Windows XP) you have to install this framework first. Net framework can be downloaded directly from the Microsoft's website.

The first component of the Net framework called common language runtime or CLR, the second component is the compiler for several programming languages supported, such as VB.NET.

CLR manage code executions in .NET platform, so the code can be directed to a certain version of the runtime environment.

NET framework also provides several classes that can be used by the developer. Framework or class library has a version and operating target on specific CLR. With this library, you can develop an application that targets specific version of the Dot Net.

On several occasions, CLR and Net framework are similar. For example Net Framework 1.0 run on CLR version 1.0. But in another case, they can have a different version, for example, VB compiler on version 10, while the Net Framework has latest version that targets older CLR.

It's also similar to Visual studio, for example, VS 2003 focus on Net 1.1 while VS.NET 2002 focus on NET 1.0. VS 2012 and 2013 focus on Net framework 4.5 but this version can also support previous versions of Net Framework.

For ASP.NET, Microsoft chooses not to change for Net 3.0 version. The bottom line is visual studio will encapsulate every technology needed and makes programmer's task easier.

1.5 History of Visual Basic.NET

The visual basic programming language has evolved significantly since a decade ago. But actually, the development of VB programming languages has been initiated since 1964.

Visual basic was amongst the most popular programming languages. Report from an independent source even concludes that visual basic is the most popular programming languages on earth. Basically, because it's easy to understand, easy to learn.

1.5.1 Root of Visual Basic

Visual basic now is a full-fledged object-oriented programming language. But actually, at the beginning, BASIC was just an ordinary high-level language that makes it easy to program for ordinary people.

In the mid of 1960s, a computer was very expensive and heavy. It was only used for special purpose processing. On that era, the processing technique was batch processing. That is the computer only process one task each time, and the next task will be done after the current task processing finished.

But at the end of the 1960s, new computer technologies emerged. Faster and cheaper. With the advancement of processor's ability, computer can be idle without any job. Since this era, processing ability provided more abundant power than what the task needed.

The programming language in batch processing era, designed for special purposes task. The same as the PC as the program's platform, eg: for scientific calculation, business data processing, or just a simple text editing program.

BASIC language initially designed by John G Kemeny and Thomas E Kurtz. Its aim was to provide access for a programmer who has no IT background.

At first, BASIC was implemented for a couple of students in Dartmouth College. BASIC was designed to simplify students to write a program for Dartmouth Time-Sharing System.

BASIC language designed to overcome the complexity of existing available programming languages. That's why BASIC comes with a new design specially addressed for beginners. For peoples with no technical background and have a less mathematic background.

With the emergence of several BASIC dialects, the BASIC language created by Kemeny and Kurtz was named Dartmouth BASIC.

BASIC stands for **Beginner's All-Purpose Symbolic Instruction Code**. The invention of basic was a revolutionary move in that era. Because everyone who wants to use a computer, have to write his/her own codes. And the one that can do this was only experts.

And since BASIC used interpreted language, people with non-IT background can easily use this programming language. Here are some BASIC language features:

- Very easy to use, especially for beginners.
- Can be used as a general purpose programming language.
- New features can be added, including features for advanced users. But still, maintain the simplicity.
- Interactive.
- Error messages easily understood.
- Quick response time, suitable for small programs.
- Don't demand an advanced knowledge of computer's hardware.
- Users don't need to understand how operating system works.

BASIC languages development, based on FORTRAN II and ALGOL 60, but slightly modified to enable time-sharing. Before

BASIC, Dartmouth College already have DARSIMCO (1956), DOPE, and DART (a simplified version of FORTRAN II).

Initially, BASIC focused on supporting mathematical works with arithmetic metric as a batch language but then support string functions on 1965.

BASIC implemented initially on General Electrics GE-265 mainframe that supports multi terminals.

1.5.2 Personal Computer Era

BASIC initially was not recognized as a popular programming language, but everything changed since Micro Instrumentation Telemetry System (MITS) released Altair 8800 on 1975 which is a BASIC-inside computer, BASIC started to show an increasing number of users.

In that era, most programming languages need lots of memory. And BASIC is a simple programming language. With a slow access because of using tape and inadequate text editor, BASIC became a very sexy programming language.

One of the initial implementation of the BASIC language for Intel 8080 processor is Altair 8800 called Tiny BASIC. This BASIC implementation was written by Dr. Li-Chen Wang which is then rewritten to run on Altair by Dennis Allison. The source code of this program published later in 1976 in Dr. Dobb's Journal.

In 1975, MITS released Altair BASIC, developed by William Henry Gates III and Paul Allen of Microsoft. The first Altair version was developed by Gates, Allen, and Monte Davidoff together.

The advent of Microsoft BASIC on most platforms makes PC sales increases. And finally Microsoft BASIC become a standard language used by Apple II computer that uses MPU Mostek 6502.

Until 1979, Microsoft has licensed lots of IBM BASIC, a BASIC language interpreter they developed. A version of IBM BASIC was put in a ROM chip in the IBM PC, so the PC will be able to start immediately BASIC programming sessions if there is no floppy disk inserted.

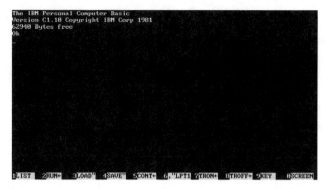

Figure 1.35 IBM Basic, one of most popular old basic version

Because BASIC grow popular. Many developers develop another version of BASIC. For example, BBC releases BBC BASIC by Acorn Computers, Ltd.

BBC BASIC has some distinctive features, such as structures for keywords. It also has an integrated assembler. BBC BASIC was amongst the best dialect of BASIC.

Figure 1.36 One of the initial version of Basic, MSX Basic

Here is some BASIC language implementation:

```
10 INPUT "Whats your name: ", U$
20 PRINT "Halo "; U$
30 INPUT "How many characters * do you want to display: ", N
40 S$ = ""
50 FOR I = 1 TO N
60 S$ = S$ + "*"
70 NEXT I
80 PRINT S$
90 INPUT "Do you want to add again? ", A$
100 IF LEN(A$) = 0 THEN GOTO 90
```

```
110 A$ = LEFT$(A$, 1)
120 IF A$ = "Y" OR A$ = "y" THEN GOTO 30
130 PRINT "Good bye"; U$
140 END
```

1.5.3 Visual Basic Era

BASIC languages becoming more popular on visual operating system era. Microsoft introduced Visual Basic ("VB"), on 1991. The syntax quite familiar because based on legendary BASIC language.

The programming language doesn't need to be fully defined such as CLI (*command line interface*) version because the visual programming now uses "drag and drop". It makes developer tasks easier and the program can use the visual component such as button and scrollbar.

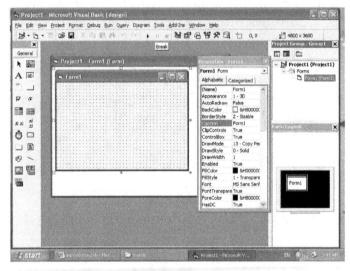

Figure 1.37 Visual basic 6, one of the most popular classic visual basic that still has many active developers right now

Even if BASIC initially addressed for beginners. VB also used by lots of professional programmers that develop applications for small and medium enterprises.

1.6 Run First Program

A recently created project only has one form. This is a raw form, and if you run the project, this form will be the first window of your program. Here are steps to run a program in visual basic.net:

1. Click on the form, the surrounding of the form will have a thin dotted line. It's an indication that the form is selected.

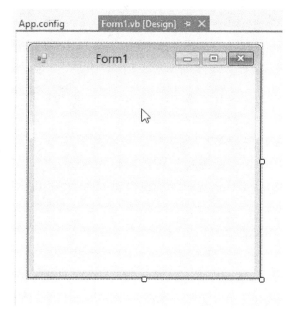

Figure 1.38 The surrounding of the form has thin dotted line

2. The Titlebar of the form contains text "Form1", "Form2" etc. You can change this by clicking on the form, then find Text properties on properties panel.

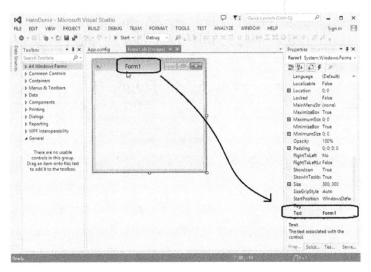

Figure 1.39 Change the Text Properties of the panel

3. You can change this with strings variable you like.

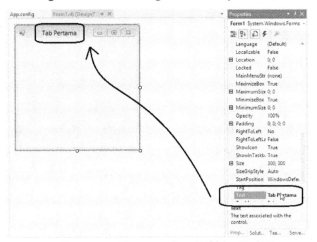

Figure 1.40 Changing property text in Properties

4. The result, the title bar will change its text.

5. You can also add an object from toolbox by double click on the object or drag and drop the object to the form.

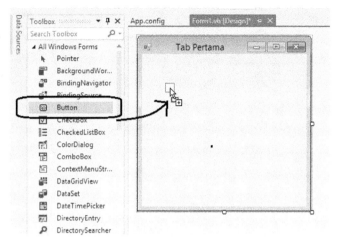

Figure 1.41 Insert object component from toolbox into the form

6. It will create an object named Button1 and with text Button1.

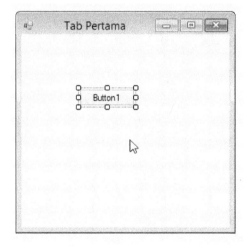

Figure 1.42 A new button inserted into the form

7. To change the properties of the button, click on the button and find **Text** properties on **Properties** panel.

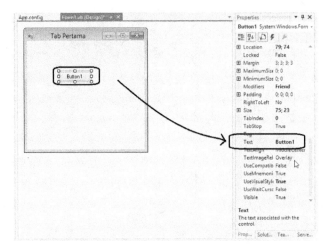

Figure 1.43 Find the Text properties on a button

8. To change the text, just change the string inside the Text properties.

Figure 1.44 Change the text properties

9. You are advised to change the properties of each object. This will make the code more readable. For the button, the standard name is Button1 but you can also change it with other text strings.

Figure 1.45 Change button name

10. If you change the name, no changes on display will occur, the changes only applied to **Properties** panel.

Figure 1.46 The changes of name properties

11. Text properties will be shown in Design panel, while the Name properties will not be changed because name properties won't appeared on the form.

Figure 1.47 Form shown after the text and name properties changed

12.   To run the program, click **F5** or click **Start debugging** button on the toolbar.

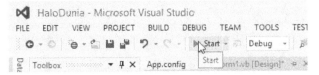

Figure 1.48 Click the Start button to run the program

13.   The program will run nicely for the first time

Figure 1.49 Initial appearance of the program

14.   When the button clicked, nothing happened. It's because you (the programmer) haven't inserted a single code to control the action of the click of the button.

1.7 Inserting Control Object Item

If you have a knowledge of Java programming or Android programming, you will meet an object called widget. In VB.net, a widget is identical with control object item.

Every control object in vb net has specific functions, for examples: a button will accept a click, a textBox will accept the string of texts, a scrollbar will receive a scroll from a user. Groupbox will group control object items, etc.

Here are an example of inserting control objects on a form:

1. Click on **Project** menu then click **Add new item** menu.

2. Appear a new **Add new item** window.

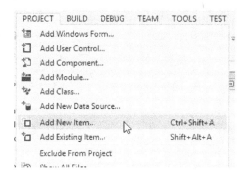

Figure 1.50 Add New Item Window

3. Choose Windows Form.

Figure 1.51 Insert new Windows Form item

4. Click **Add** button to add this item.

5. On Design view, a new form will emerge.

Figure 1.52 A new form emerge with name = Form2

6. You can also see the Solution Explorer has Form2.vb. This is another proof that a new control object item has already inserted.

Figure 1.53 Newly inserted item in Solution Explorer

7. To show an item already inserted. Double click on the item name in solution explorer panel, you'll see an active form.

Figure 1.54 Newly inserted form activated

8. To close an item, hover your pointer over the tab of the item, and click the [X] button like this picture below:

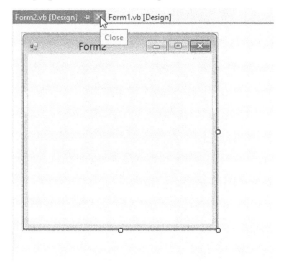

Figure 1.55 Click Close button to close an item

9. You can also add a module. The module is a place to write codes or to define a function or to declare global variable. To add module, click Project > Add module.

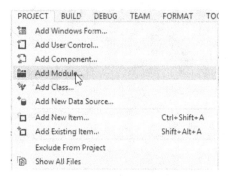

Figure 1.56 Menu Add Module

10.   Insert module name on **Name** textbox, and choose **Module** on category item.

Figure 1.57 Insert module name on Name textbox in Add new item window

11.   The center panel will display the new module added and the Solution explorer indicates a new item with type **Module** exists.

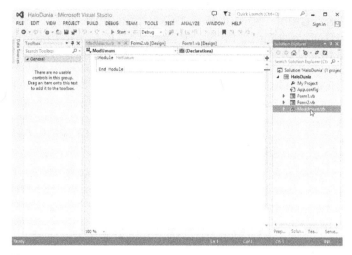

Figure 1.58 A new module successfully inserted indicated by ModUmum.vb on Solution explorer

1.8 Visual Studio Project Types

A visual studio.net projects can be more than one type. Here are amongst the visual studio project types:

- Windows: To create application that runs on local computer on CLR.

- Web: To create a project related to web platform, including web service.

- Office: This is Visual Studio Tools For Office. This is a net application hosted inside Office. VS contains some templates that can target office 2010, 2013 or previous version such as Office 2007

- Cloud Service: This is a project to target Windows Azure development environment. This project implemented on cloud and has special implementation.

- Reporting: This project enables you to create Reports application.

- Sharepoint: To create share point project, including Web Part, Share Point Workflow, and Business Data Catalog. VS 2010 above has solid support toward SharePoint technology.

- Silverlight: To create a Silverlight project. Almost similar to Macromedia Flash technology, but this one created by Microsoft.

- Test: This can be used by visual studio team suite. Contains templates for Visual basic unit test.

- WCF: To create Windows Communication Foundation (WCF) project.

- Workflow: To create Workflow Foundation (WF). Contains template that can connect with SharePoint Workflow engine.

1.9 Inserting The Code

On the previous subchapter, you have inserted some visual object items onto the program. But the program does nothing when you click a button, simply because you haven't inserted any codes into the program.

Codes are the logics behind the program. You are commanding the program to act using the codes you write. What you can do using codes can be very diverse. From just as simple as displaying alert message via a message box, until creating reports or database operations.

Codes in vb net are event-drive codes, that is codes will be called/activated only if the event related to the codes triggered.

Here are steps to insert the code into the program:

1. We use button from the previous example, Double click the button.

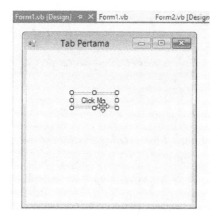

Figure 1.59 Double-click the button

2. A Code editor window will be displayed. You'll see a procedure initiated with "Private Sub" and Ended with "End Sub". Between them, you can insert the code.

Figure 1.60 Tampilan editor code

3. The codes will be like this, this will with the object's name properties.

```
Public Class Form1


    Private Sub btnClickMe_Click(sender As Object, e As
EventArgs) Handles btnClickMe.Click

    End Sub
End Class
```

4. In the middle of the codes, you can insert new lines of codes. This time with ' character that means texts after that is comments and will not be processed by vb.net compiler.

Figure 1.61 Inserting few lines of codes

5. For example, you can insert a message box by clicking MsgBox. During writing M S G you may see a list box appears, this is called IntelliSense to help you type the codes to minimize errors.

Figure 1.62 Intellisense/autocomplete to ease the codes insertion

6. Then insert the codes. You may change the codes' texts

```
Private Sub btnClickMe_Click(sender As Object, e As Even-
tArgs) Handles btnClickMe.Click
        'you can write any codes here
        ' these texts are comments, will not compile
        MsgBox("Let's Learn VB.NET", MsgBoxStyle.Information,
"Information")

    End Sub
```

7. Save the project using **CTRL + S** on your keyboard. This will save your codes into your project. If you haven't saved the codes, an asterisk (*) will emerge on the right of your tab name. If you save the project, this asterisk character will disappear.

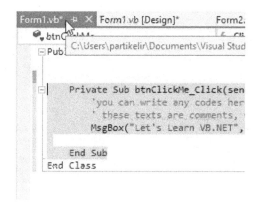

*Figure 1.63 Asterisk sign * means the codes haven't been saved*

8. You can now run the program by clicking F5 button on your keyboard or click Debugging button. A window will appear.

Figure 1.64 Click the button

9. A message box will emerge with the text corresponds to the codes you inserted before.

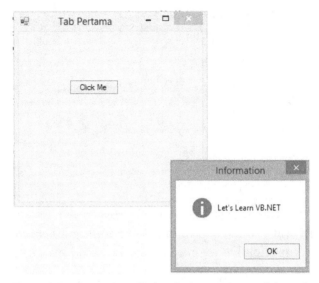

Figure 1.65 Messagebox displayed after you inserted the codes

10.   Click the **Stop Debugging** button to stops the running of the program.

CHAPTER 2 UNDERSTANDING KEYWORDS AND SYNTAXES OF VB.NET

Visual basic.net keywords and syntaxes were similar with the previous version of visual basic. There are two terms in object-oriented programming, including visual basic.net:

1. Method: generic name for command in visual basic. The Sub and Function are types of Method.

2. Instance: When a class created, the object created was the instance from the class definition.

There are some keywords and descriptions you need to understand while programming on OOP:

Keywords	Descriptions
Namespace	Classes collection that provides related abilities, for example, System.Drawing contains classes related with graphic.
Class	Definition of object, including properties (variable) and method that can be a Sub or a Function.
Sub	A method that contains commands, enable data transferred as parameter and provide scope inside local variable but doesn't return value.
Function	A method that contains commands, enable data transferred as parameter and provide scope

	inside local variables and commands.
Return	Terminate Sub or Function currently executed. Can be combined with return value for function.
Dim	Declare and define new variable
New	Create new instance from object.
Nothing	To indicate that a variable has no value. Similar with null in other programming languages, or in database.
Me	Reference to object inside the scope where the method executed.
Console	An application type that runs on command line. Console app in dot net usually needed for testing purpose only. The console also refers to class that manages command window and can read and write text data.
Module	Block of codes but not a class, can contain Sub or Function method. Used when there are only one code or data needed in the memory.

2.1 Compiler Options

Before you type codes, you need to set compiler options. There are many compiler options setup you can choose:

- Option Explicit: This option doesn't change from the previous version of visual basic. If it's activated or enabled. It will make sure that variable declared explicitly. If you use Option Strict, this setting won't be problem, because compiler doesn't recognize the type of the undeclared variables. Basically, you don't have to use Option Explicit, unless you build a pure dynamic solution, where compilation time for typing unavailable.

- Option Strict: When this option enabled, compiler will decide type of each variable. And if assignment between two variables needs type conversion, eg: from integer to boolean, this conversion should be expressed explicitly.

- Option Compare: This option helps to make sure whether string has to be compared to string binary, or character has to be compared as text. Text comparison needs system to compare binary value saved internally before compared.

- Option Infer: This option exists since VS 2008 and added because of LINQ requirement. When you execute LINQ statement, you will return data table that can't be typed in statement Advanced.

2.2 Variable

Variable in programming language is a place to store information in computer memories. You can imagine a variable like an empty box, you can save some value in variable.

To add two numbers, for example, you just write the first number on an empty paper and put the paper on the empty box, then you write the second number on an empty paper and put the second paper on the empty box.

In visual basic.net, this will be identical to this:

```
Dim number1 As Integer
Dim number2 As Integer
number1 = 3
number2 = 5
```

Codes above are codes in visual basic.net that describe how Visual Basic Net create and define variables.

Below are the explanations on several keywords used while defining variables:

Dim

Dim stands for "Dimension". This keyword used to declare variable type. By using this keyword, you are declaring a variable in visual basic.

number1

This can be compared with an empty box, label and it's content. This is variable. In other words, this is your storage area, the place where you save your value.

After the DIM, visual basic will name your variable. You can name the variable with everything you like. But there are some reserved words you may not use.

As Integer

This keyword describe the variable type. Here, you tell visual basic that the variable will be an integer. This will define the box's size, different type will make the size of the variable different.

number1 = 3

The "=" character means you insert something into your variable. Here, you tell visual basic to set 3 to variable number1.

2.3 Variable Types

Variable has many types. In VB.net, each variable type will have its own scope. And can consume spaces in computer memory.

Boolean

A boolean variable can contain True and False data. Inside the visual basic, the value saved as number 1 and 0 it represents **True** and **False**.

A boolean value used as a conditional statement to determine whether some parts of the codes will be executed or not. It's for controlling the flow of the program.

Char

Char value contains one character, eg: "B". Char value can be any characters. It can span from 0 to 65.553. It can also be used to save data from ASCII table. Eg: Z can be used on char variable and number 90 used in variable location.

Byte

Byte variable contains positive number from 0 to 255. Because the range is very small, you have to use byte variable wisely, if this variable inserted with negative value, or value bigger than 255, this will cause an error.

Date

Date in visual basic can save date and time. Date should be inserted on #mm/dd/yyyy# format. For example May 23, 2016, will be declared as #5/23/2016#.

Visual basic use some mechanisms to work with Date variable. For example to count six months after today.

Decimal

A decimal variable can save up to 29 decimal places. If you use decimal number, it's okay using this variable. If you use nondecimal number, then use integer.

Double

Double variable used to save value that needs up to 28 decimal places. Double can be positive values from range 4.94065645841246544E-324 to 1.79769313486231570E+308 negative values from -1.79769313486231570E+30 to - 4.94065645841246544E-324.

Double variable usually used to develop a scientific application and rarely used by regular developer.

Integer

Integer variable used to save number between -2,147,483,648 until 2,147,483,648. This integer variable can't save values that have fractional value/decimal. If the value has fraction, it will be rounded automatically.

Object

Object variable is a variable type that can be used to save all types of data. Because of this flexibility, object variable consumes more memory space than other variable types. It's not recommended to be used. Use specific type that you need.

Long

Long variable used to save all numbers ranged from - 9,233,372,036,854,775,808 to 9,233,372,036,854,775,807.

Short

Short variable save number ranged from -32,768 to 32,767.

String

String variable saves characters that can construct word or statements. String variable always opened and closed with quotation marks ("). For example "Hellow" or "Hellow, how are you?".

Visual basic provides mechanisms to work with and manipulate strings. Table below details variables that hold number data type. :

Name in VB	Size	Range
SByte	8 bits (1 byte)	-128 to 127
Byte	8 bits (1 byte)	0 to 255
Short	16 bits (2 bytes)	-32,768 to 32,767
UShort	16 bits (2 bytes)	0 to 65,535
Integer	32 bits (4 bytes)	-2,147,483,648 to 2,147,483,647
UInteger	32 bits (4 bytes)	0 to 4,294,967,295
Long	64 bits (8 bytes)	-9,223,372,036,854,775,808 to 9,223,372,036,854,775,807
ULong	64 bits (8 bytes)	0 to 18,446,744,073,709,551,615

Variable types for floating points:

Name in VB	Size	Precision	Range
Single	32 bit (4 bytes)	7 digits	1.5×10^{-45} to 3.4×10^{38}
Double	64 bit (8 bytes)	15-16 digits	5.0×10^{-324} to 1.7×10^{308}
Decimal	128 bit (16 bytes)	28-29 decimals	1.0×10^{-28} to 7.9×10^{28}

Other predefined:

Name in VB	Size (bit)	Range
Char	16 bit (2 bytes)	One Unicode symbol ranges 0 to 65,535.
Boolean	32 bit (4 bytes)	True or False
Object	32/64 bit (4/8 bytes)	Platform dependent (the reference to object).
Date	64 bit (8 bytes)	January 1, 0001 12:00:00 AM to December 31, 9999 11:59:59 PM
String	80 + [16 * length] bit (10 + [2 * length] byte)	Unicode strings with 2,147,483,647 characters maximum length.

To allocate a numeric value, you can use equal sign "=". To allocate a certain numeric value to variable already declared, yo could use variable = certain_value.

For string and char variables, you can use quotation mark:

```
MystrVariable= "Some strings"
cMyhrVariable= "À"
```

For date/time, you can use hash/pound between value, by using this format #<month>/<day>/<year> <hour>:<minute>:<second> <AM|PM>#. For example:

```
MyDateVariable= #7/4/2016 12:01:50 PM#
```

For other types, you don't have to use anything.

```
myBytVariable = 1
mysbytVariable = -2
MyshrtVariable = 10S
MyushrtVariable = 10US
MyintVariable = 100
YouruIntVariable= 100UI
YourlnGVariable= 1000L
YouruLngVariable= 1000UL
sngVariable = 1.234F
dblVariable= 1.567R
decVariable = 1234567.89D
boolVariable = True
objctVariable = New Object
```

You can also allocate value to variable on its declaration, for example:

```
Dim myVariable As String = "Another String Values"
```

Visual Basic will allocate value from right variable to the left variable. The variable on the left will take the value from the right variable. While the right variable's value won't change.

Tutorial steps below will demonstrate how to use string value:

1. Create new project for chapter two, name it, then insert form, and change the title of the form.

Figure 2.1 New project with new title

2. Create a button, we'll use the click event from the button to trigger our code.

Figure 2.2 Creating a button

3. Double click on the button, and enter this code:

```
Dim question, YourName As String
question = "What's your name?"
YourName = InputBox(question)
MsgBox("Your name is : " + YourName)

End Sub
```

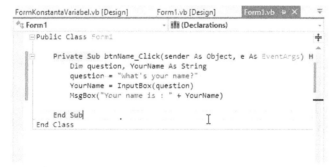

Figure 2.3 Codes to display InputBox

4. From codes above, there are two DIMs used to declare Question and YourName variables. Both of this variables are string.

5. Question variable then inserted with the string "What's your name?"

6. Later, Question variable used to show inputBox.

7. The inputted strings from inputBox will be entered to a variable YourName and displayed on the MsgBox.

8. Run the program, and click the button.

Figure 2.4 Click on the button to trigger ButtonClick event

9. An input box emerges and asks your name, insert a name and click **OK**.

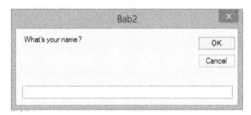

Figure 2.5 An input box to receive input from user

10.   After you entered an information, the information will be entered to a variable.

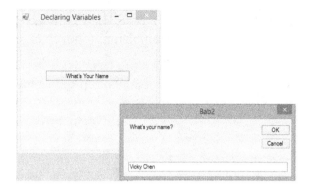

Figure 2.6 Inputting string text

11. And you'll find the string displayed in a message box.

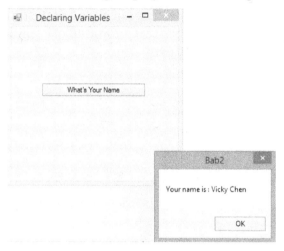

Figure 2.7 Message box displays inputted text string

12. There is a new keyword "InputBox". This keyword is a Function. What is a function? A function is statements that do a certain action and can be processed by the vb net compiler. Function also return value to the program.

13. The value returned by the function then inserted to the variable or can be allocated to other properties of a certain object. A function can also have arguments, for example, the InputBox on this tutorial needs a text argument.

2.4 Constant

Basically, constant similar to the variable. It contains a value. The difference is the value in constant cannot be changed. Constant declared using the keyword "Const".

Constant also use data type. This is an example on how to declare a constant:

```
Const myConstant As String = "This text is a constant"
```
And:

```
Const MyPi As Single = 3.14159265F
```
Constant really useful if your program regularly needs to access constant value. For example, when counting area of a circle, you can use constant Pi. You may use constant when dealing with a function such as Sin, Cos, Tan, Arctan, etc.

1. Create a new form still on the project you created for Chapter 2, Right-click on the project name in Solution Explorer, then click menu **Add > Windows Form**.

Figure 2.8 Click Add to add a new windows form to existing project for chapter 2

2. Enter the new form's **Name**, click **Add**.

Figure 2.9 Create new form to demonstrate constant

3. Enter 2 textboxes, 2 labels, and 1 button. The first textbox used to enter circle's radius, and the second textbox will display the result of the calculation.

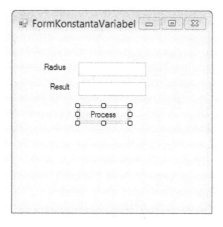

Figure 2.10 Entering 2 textboxes, 2 labels and 1 button to the form

4. Change textboxes name on the properties window.

5. Change the name for the button too.

6. Double click on the button, and then insert codes below:

```
Const pi As Double = 3.14159265
    Dim area As Double
    Dim radius As Double
    radius = Me.txtRadius.Text
    area = pi * radius * radius
    Me.txtResult.Text = area.ToString
```

7. In the codes, constant pi defined as double. It's a type for real number. Both the area and radius also defined as double.

Figure 2.11 Inserting codes for calculating area for circle

8. Since the newly added form is not startup form, you have to make it as the default form. Right click on the project chapter 2 then clicks **Properties.**

Figure 2.12 Click Properties menu on context menu from Project Chapter 2

9. Set startup form to the newly added form, and then click F5 to run the program.

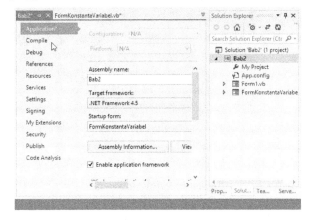

Figure 2.13 Change startup form to newly added form

10.   Wait for the program to run.

Figure 2.14 Program for demonstrating constant runs smoothly

11.   Insert the circle's radius on the first textbox and click the button to calculate.

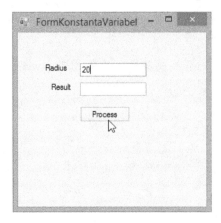

Figure 2.15 Inserting radius

12 Click **Calculate**, the circle's area will be calculated and displayed in the second textbox.

Figure 2.16 Circle's area already calculated

2.5 Array

The array is one of the variable types. But the array is not a regular variable, since it can handle multi-values. Values can be saved in a list. If you declare an array variable as an integer. That array variable can handle more than one integer values.

Here is an example:

```
Dim MyArray(5) As Integer
```
It will create an array with contents below:

```
Index       Data
00          Empty.
```

```
01          Empty.
02          Empty.
03          Empty.
04          Empty.
05          Empty.
```

So the syntax to declare an array is:

```
Dim array_name(upper_limit) As arrayType
```

Declaring an array similar with declaring a normal variable. There is only one difference, there is a limit for an array, and the first value of array started from 0.

```
Dim ArrayVariable (10) As Integer
```

This will declare an array variable with name equals ArrayVarible. It has 11 integers. Integer values will be saved on ArrayVariable(0), ArrayVarible (1),..., ArrayVariable(10).

You can also declare an array and specify the codes directly using this syntax:

```
Dim myArray() As Integer = New Integer(4) { 1, 2, 3, 4, 5 }
```

Another technique to create an array is by using codes in the modules for CLI (command line interface) application:

```
Module Module1
Sub Main()

    Dim MyArray As System.Array
    MyArray = System.Array.CreateInstance(GetType(String), 4)
    MyArray (0) = "a"
    MyArray (1) = "b"
    MyArray (2) = "c"
    MyArray (3) = "d"
    Console.WriteLine("Click Enter")
    Console.ReadLine()

End Sub
End Module
```

And the codes to Access array elements is:

```
Module Module1
Sub Main()
```

```
Dim MyArray As System.Array
MyArray = System.Array.CreateInstance(GetType(String), 4)
MyArray (0) = "a"
MyArray (1) = "b"
MyArray (2) = "c"
MyArray (3) = "d"
Console.WriteLine(MyArray.GetValue(2)) 'return c
Console.WriteLine("Click Enter")
Console.ReadLine()

End Sub
End Module
```

2.6 Conditional Statements

The logical or conditional statement used to test whether a statement's value true or false. And then execute other chunk of codes depending on the results whether true or false.

2.6.1 Some Conditional Statements

Some conditional statements supported by Visual basic.net are:

- If/Else/Endif

- If/Else If/Else/Endif

- Select Case/End Select

For example, see the codes below:

```
Dim var1 as integer
Dim var2 as integer
var1 = 4
var2 = 7
```

The standard format for IF statement is:

```
IF...THEN...ELSE...ENDIF
```

IF statement always tests the conditions and find the result true or false.

```
is var1 = 4 ........ TRUE
is var1 = 5 ........ FALSE
is var1 > 7 ........ TRUE
```

If the condition equals true, IF clause will process the upper part of the codes or in other words, codes after THEN clause. For example:

```
IF var1 = 4 THEN var2 = 10
```

If after THEN clause consists of more than one statement, it's easier and more readable to make each statement in one line. For example:

```
IF var1 = 4 THEN
   var1 = var1 + 3    'var1 will be = 7
   var2 = var2 + 1    'var2  will be = 8
Endif
```

As you see on above example IF statement can be used without ELSE clause. But when you need to define codes for the FALSE condition, ELSE clause is needed. The example:s

```
IF var1 = 4 THEN
   (execute if TRUE)
ELSE
   (execute if FALSE)
ENDIF
```

You can inverse the statement with NOT clause too. For example:

```
IF  NOT var1 = 4 THEN
    (execute if TRUE)      'if var1 = NOT 4
ELSE
    (execute if FALSE)     'if var1 = 4
ENDIF
```

To make reading the code easier, you can add parenthesis on the statement. For example:

```
IF  NOT (var1 = 4) THEN ............
```

You can also add nested IF statement, If...ElseIf...Else...EndIf. If/ElseIf statement can be used to test more than one boolean statements. If evaluated condition True, then the block of codes will be executed. If it's False, will be continued to ElseIf Clause.

ElseIF clause and Else are not obligatory in IF statement.

This is an example of the usage of If clause in vb.net:

```
Dim x As Integer
Dim y As Integer


If x = y Then
  'will be executed if x = y
ElseIf x < y Then
```

```
  'will be executed if x < y
Else
  'Will be executed if x != y and x not < y
End If
```

The next clause in a conditional statement is Select Case. You can read the example below:

```
Dim CPUs as Integer
Select Case CPUs
     Case 0
          'No CPU!
     Case 1
          'Single CPU
     Case 2
          'Dual CPUs
     Case 4
          'Quad CPU
     Case 3, 5 To 8
          '3, 5, 6, 7, 8 CPUs
     Case Else
          'More than 8 CPUs
End Select
```

2.7 Operators

Logical Operators used to combine more than one boolean values and return the result from the combination. You can combine boolean values by using rules on Karnaugh Map:

And	1	0
1	1	0
0	0	0

Or	1	0
1	1	1
0	1	0

Xor	1	0
1	0	1
0	1	0

Not	1	0
	0	1

Figure 2.17 Karnaugh Map

Arithmetical operators, to do some mathematical operation.

Operator	Function
^	Exponential
-	Negation, to reverse the plus/minus from a number. Eg: from -1 to 1, vice versa.
*	Multiplication
/	Division
\	Integer division
Mod	Modulus
+	Addition
-	Subtraction

Concatenation operators:

Operator	Function

+	Concatenate string
&	Concatenate string

Comparison operators can be used to compare two values, and then return whether the result of the comparison is True or False.

Operator	Function
=	Equals
<>	Not equals
<	Less than
>	More than
>=	More than or equals
<=	Less than or equals

The tutorial below will demonstrate how to make a program that uses arithmetical operator:

1. Create a new form on existing project Chapter 2 project and click **Add**.

Figure 2.18 Create new form on existing project Chapter 2

2. Insert 5 labels, 3 textboxes and 1 list box. Listbox will be used to choose arithmetical operator used.

3. Insert 1 button to process the operation.

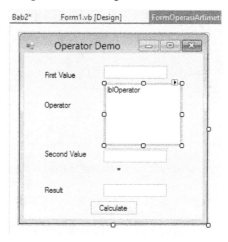

Figure 2.19 Inserting objects

4. Change the ListBox name with lbOperator, then click **Items** (**Collection**) and click the ellipsis button [...].

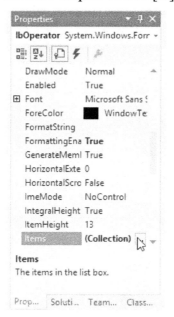

Figure 2.20 Clicking the ellipsis button in lbOperator

5. Insert some arithmetical operators then click **OK**.

Figure 2.21 Inserting arithmetical operators on list box's items

6. The appearance of Operator Listbox will be updated.

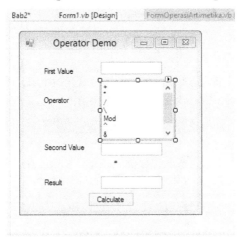

Figure 2.22 Operator list box updated

7. Double click on the button, then insert codes below;

```
Dim varA As Integer = Me.txtFirstValue.Text
Dim varB As Integer = Me.txtSecondValue.Text

If Me.lbOperator.Text = "+" Then
    Me.txtResult.Text = varA + varB
ElseIf Me.lbOperator.Text = "*" Then
    Me.txtResult.Text = varA * varB
ElseIf Me.lbOperator.Text = "/" Then
    Me.txtResult.Text = varA / varB
```

```
ElseIf Me.lbOperator.Text = "\" Then
    Me.txtResult.Text = varA \ varB
ElseIf Me.lbOperator.Text = "Mod" Then
    Me.txtResult.Text = varA Mod varB
ElseIf Me.lbOperator.Text = "^" Then
    Me.txtResult.Text = varA ^ varB
ElseIf Me.lbOperator.Text = "&" Then
    Me.txtResult.Text = varA & varB
ElseIf Me.lbOperator.Text = "-" Then
    Me.txtResult.Text = varA - varB
End If
```

8. Change the startup form for the existing project to this newly added form.

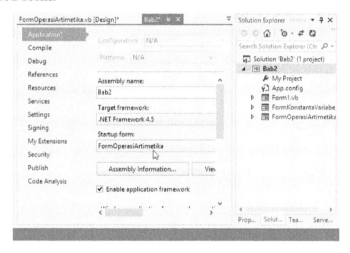

Figure 2.23 Changing the startup form for the project

9. Run the program, the form ready to do some arithmetical operations.

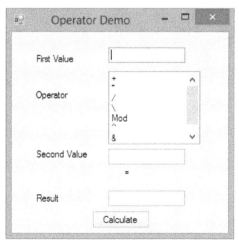

Figure 2.24 Arithmetical

10. Enter the operands then choose the operator in Operator list box.

11.   Click Calculate button to calculate.

Figure 2.25 Addition operation

12.   You can change the operator to / to perform a division operation.

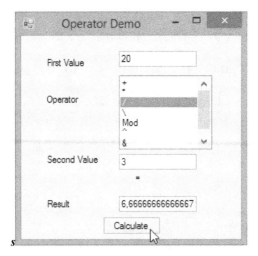

Figure 2.26 Division operation

13.   Change the operator to * to do multiplication

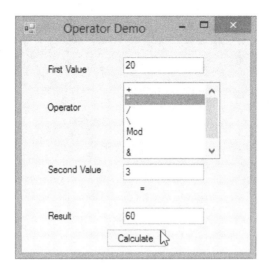

Figure 2.27 Multiplication operation

14.   Change \ to find integer division.

*Figure 2.28 Integer division using *

15.   Change Mod to find the modulus division.

Figure 2.29 Modulus

16. Change the operator to ^ to do the exponential operation.

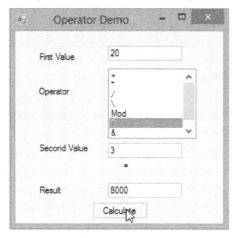

Figure 2.30 Exponential operation using ^

17. Change operator to & to do concatenation operation.

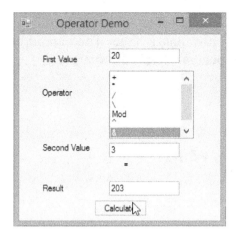

Figure 2.31 Concatenation operator

18. Change operator to – to do subtraction operation.

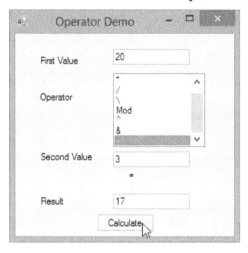

Figure 2.32 Subtraction operation using -

2.7 Repetition Using Loop

Ability to do repetition is what makes computer greater than a human being. The computer can do one million repetitions without boring and lost focus. There are many repetitions in VB.net

2.7.1 Do...Loop Until

Do...Loop Until is a loop that will always run and will stop if the tested condition becoming a True. The condition will be checked each time a loop occurs. Here's the syntax:

```
Do
     ' Loop codes here
Loop Until condition
```

2.7.2 Do...Loop While

Do...Loop While is a loop that will always run and will stop if the tested condition becoming a False. Here's the syntax:

```
Do
     ' Loop codes here
Loop While condition
```

2.7.3 Do Until...Loop

Do Until...Loop is similar with Do...Loop Until. The difference is the tested condition checked at the beginning, not at the end.

```
Do Until condition
     ' Loop codes here
Loop
```

2.7.4 Loop Do While...

Do While... is similar with Do...Loop While. And also similar with Do Until..., where the tested condition checked at the beginning of the iteration. Here's the syntax:

```
Do While condition
     ' loop codes here
Loop
```

2.7.5 Loop For

Loop For will do repetition where the counter determined after For clause. Here's the syntax:

```
For a = 1 To 10
     ' Loop codes here
Next
```

Codes above will loop 10 times since the first iteration.

Here's the second loop:

```
For a = 10 To 1 Step -1
    ' Loop codes here
Next
```

The second codes will also loop 10x, but the counter starts from 10 and decrease one by one.

Another example:

```
For a = 11 To 20
    ' Loop codes here
Next
```

It also loops 10 times. The counter will at 11 then stops when it reaches 20.

2.7.6 Loop For Each

For Each loop will iterate every index from an array or from another object. Here's the example:

```
Dim arr As Integer() = { 1, 2, 3 }
Dim i As Integer
For Each i In arr
    ' Loop will be done as long as
    ' an integer exists in arr, eg: 1, 2, or 3
Next
```

2.8 Procedure and Functions

In visual basic, and in all programming languages, there is procedure and functions. The procedure is a unit to group codes to do some action according to the algorithm given by the programmer. The procedure usually doesn't give return values.

In visual basic, a procedure will be placed between Private Sub and End Sub. Private Sub is the opening clause, and End sub is Closing class.

Here's an example of procedure:

```
Private Sub Tell_Me_your_age()
Dim YourAge as Single
YourAge= 5
MsgBox ("You are " + YourAge + "years old")
End Sub
```

The procedure above use Private clause that means the procedure's scope is private. But a procedure can also have public scope. A private procedure can only be accessed by other codes in common class. While the public procedure can be accessed from other class.

Here's an example of a public procedure:

```
Public Sub Tell_Me_Your_Age ()
Dim YourAge as Single
YourAge = 5
MsgBox ("You Are " + YourAge + "years old")
End Sub
```

You can call the procedure using Call clause. For example:

```
Private Sub ShowAge()
'Calling previous procedure
Call Tell_Me_Your_Age()
End Sub
```

If the procedure exists in other module or another form, you must mention the name of the class where the procedure exists. For example:

```
 Private Sub ShowAge()
'Calling previous procedure
Call PublicMod.Tell_Me_Your_Age ()
End Sub
```

Function is similar to a procedure, as a matter of fact, the function is a procedure but not a regular procedure or you may also say beyond procedure. The function is a procedure because function does some actions just like procedure and defined in a certain unit. The difference is that function usually return a value while a procedure doesn't return anything.

For a Function, the opening should have a Function declaration, for example:

```
Function YourAge (ByVal bornYear As Integer) As Integer
Dim Age As Integer
Age = 2015 - bornYear
Return Age
End Function
```

To call function, the method is similar to calling procedure. You could use Call clause and enter the variable you want to process.

For example:

```
Private Sub BerapaUmurnya
```

```
Call YourAge (1983)
End Sub
```

CHAPTER 3 DEALING WITH CONTROL OBJECTS

Every control object in vb.net has specific properties and usage. Visual programming is dealing with how to manage control objects and make the control objects behave as intended.

To be able to practice techniques in this chapter, you have to create a new project for Chapter 3. Here's how:

1. Click on **File > New Project**.

Figure 3.1 Click File > New Project menu

2. Choose Windows Forms Application, and enter the name of the project that will contain all tutorials in this Chapter3 on the Name text box. Click OK.

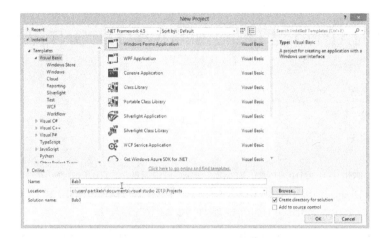

Figure 3.2 Selecting Windows Forms Application

3. The new project will be displayed in the main window of visual studio, with one default form.

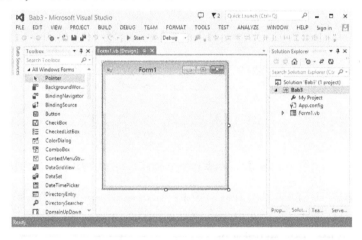

Figure 3.3 New Project for chapter 3 already created

3.1 Labels

Label is an object used to display text strings, but cannot receive input by the user. If you want to edit label's content, you can use vb codes or change the text's properties on **Properties** panel.

Here's a demonstration on how to use a label in visual basic.net program.

1. Open the toolbox panel, then click **Common Controls > Label**. Drag it to the form.

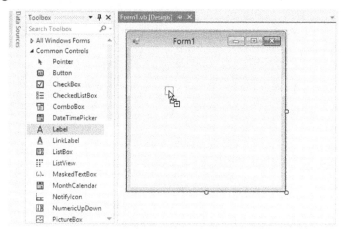

Figure 3.4 Click on Labels

2. Enter three labels, Label1, Label2, and Label3.

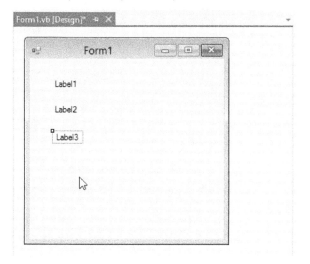

Figure 3.5 Entering three labels onto the form

3. Select Label1, open Properties panel, and find Text properties:

Figure 3.6 Find Text Properties

4. Change the text properties to "Name".

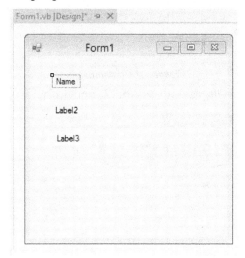

Figure 3.7 Change text properties to "Name"

5. With the same method, change Label2's text property to "Address".

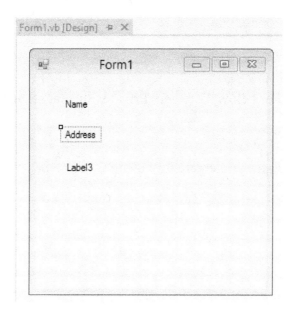

Figure 3.8 Change Label2's text property to address

6. For Label3, you can leave it untouched. We'll change it using vb net codes. Double click on the form. The code window will emerge and automatically created a procedure for handling event Form1_Load.

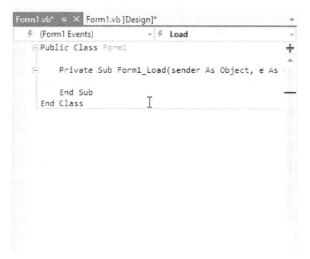

Figure 3.9 Click on the form

7. The codes will be like this:

```
Public Class Form1
```

```
    Private Sub Form1_Load(sender As Object, e As EventArgs)
Handles MyBase.Load

    End Sub
End Class
```

8. Enter codes below between Private Subclause and End Sub-clause.

```
Me.Label3.Text = "Work and Hobby"
```

9. Save the codes you entered by using CTRL + S.

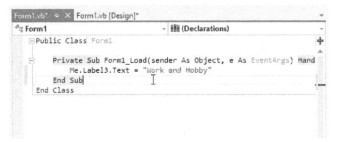

Figure 3.10 Modifying the text properties using vb.net codes

10. If you run the program, the appearance will be like this, you can see Label3 has different text, although, in the Design view, it has other text. It's because you command the vb compiler to change the label3's text during the loading of the Form.

Figure 3.11 The result of the program

3.2 Textboxes

Text boxes can display texts and receive input. Here's a demonstration on how to use a label in visual basic.net program.

1. Enter new form on the project. Right click on project's name in Solution explorer, then click **Add > New item**.

Figure 3.12 Menus to create new form of existing project

2. Add New Item window appears, choose Windows form object to add.

3. Enter the name, and click Add.

Figure 3.13 Entering new form name and type

4. In solution explorer, a new icon appears that showing the newly added form.

Figure 3.14 New text box appears

5. Change the text properties from the new form.

6. Click **TextBox** icon in the Toolbox panel to enter Toolbox object item.

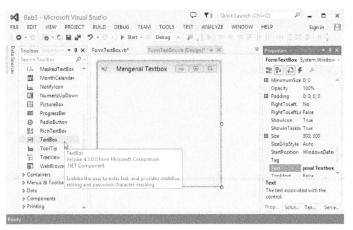

Figure 3.15 Click on the object item

7. Enter 3 textboxes.

Figure 3.16 Three text boxes inserted

8. Enter three labels with text properties: Name, Address, and Occupation.

9. Enter button, and change the button's name property with "btnProcess" and change the text with **Process**.

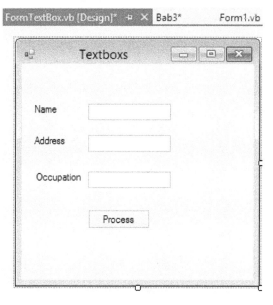

Figure 3.17 Enter three labels and button

10. Double click the button and enter codes below:

```
        Private Sub btnProses_Click(sender As Object, e As
EventArgs) Handles btnProses.Click
        MsgBox("Your Name " + Me.txtName.Text + " your address "
+ Me.txtAddress.Text + " Your occupation " +
Me.txtOccupation.Text, MsgBoxStyle.Information, "Information")
    End Sub
```

Figure 3.18 Entering codes to display message box which displays data from textbox

11. Before running the program, change startup Form to this newly added form. Right click on project's item in Solution Explorer, then click **Properties** menu.

Figure 3.19 Right click on project's icon

12.　　In Properties window, find Startup Form and choose the form for this tutorial as Startup Form.

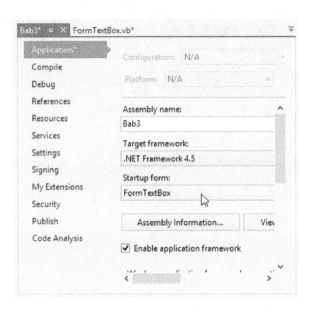

Figure 3.20 Change the Startup Form

13.   Run the program, it will display the form and the content of textbox will be null.

Figure 3.21 Form will be run

14.   Enter texts on the textbox and click Process button.

Figure 3.22 Entering texts on the textbox

15. After you clicked the button, a message box will appear showing texts inputted by the user in the textboxes before.

Figure 3.23 Texts from text boxes appeared on a message box

3.3. Menus

Menus can be used as the main menu or a context menu. All of the menus use an object called MenuStrip.

Here's a demonstration on creating menus in vb.net:

1. Enter new form, by right click on project's icon in Solution Explorer, then click **Add New item** menu, Enter new file with Windows Form type and enter the name at Name text box.

Figure 3.24 Entering new form for existing project for demonstrating Menu

2. After the form entered, change the text properties.

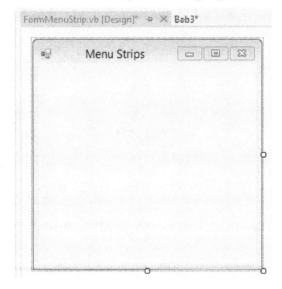

Figure 3.25 Change text properties for the form

3. Click on the MenuStrip icon in **Menus & Toolbars > Menu Strip** on Toolbox panel.

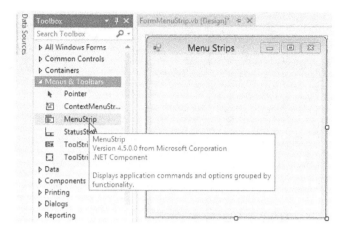

Figure 3.26 Click on Menu Strip

4. If the menu strip already entered, on the lower part of the form, will emerge an icon named MenuStrip1 and below the title bar, will emerge a box with text **Type here**.

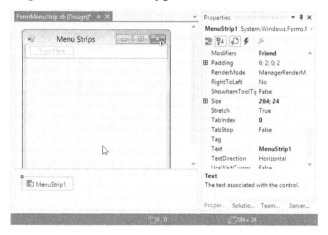

Figure 3.27 Form appearance after a MenuStrip object inserted

5. To enter menus on the menu strip, you just click Type here and type texts for the menu you want to enter.

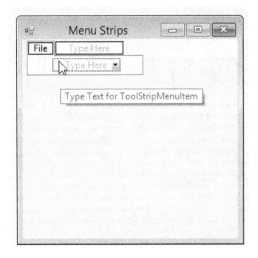

Figure 3.28 Typing "File" on submenu

6. You can add another text on another menu.

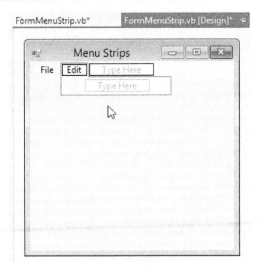

Figure 3.29 Typing "Edit"

7. You can add child menu with the same method.

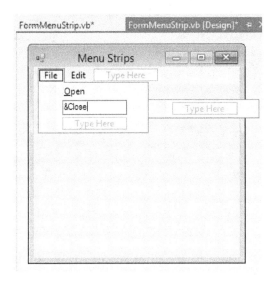

Figure 3.30 Adding child menu with the same method

8. To create a shortcut for the menu, you can use &. The alphabet that has underscore means that the menu can be accessed using ALT + alphabet.

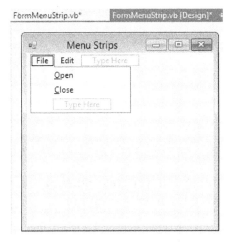

Figure 3.31 Result of the shortcut creation on menu items

9. Each menu item will have its own name depending on the text you entered.

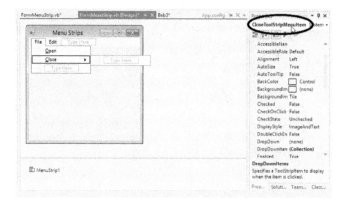

Figure 3.32 Menu item has its own name

10. To enter codes to the click event for the menu, double click on the menu item.

```
        Private Sub OpenToolStripMenuItem_Click(sender As
Object, e As EventArgs) Handles OpenToolStripMenuItem.Click

        End Sub
```

11. For example, i want to enter codes to display message box on one of the menu items.

```
            MsgBox("You want to open something?")
```

Figure 3.33 Entering codes for one of the menu item

12. Before running this program, change the project properties to make this active form as Startup Form.

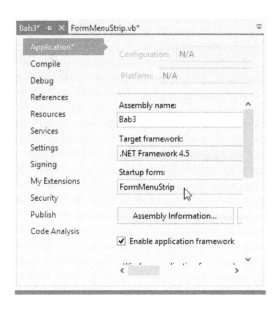

Figure 3.34 Changing the startup form to this active form

13.   Run program with F5, at the beginning, the main menu will have to menu items.

Figure 3.35 Main menu will have two menu items

14. If you click File menu, the child menus appear.

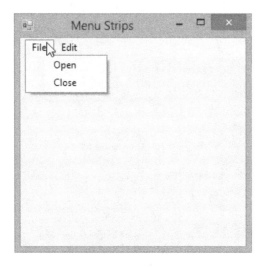

Figure 3.36 Child menus of the File menu appear if you click the File menu

15.   To Access the shortcut, you could click ALT button on your keyboard before clicking a button.

Figure 3.37 Shortcut for menus appeared

16. If you click the menu item that has codes inside it, an action will be done.

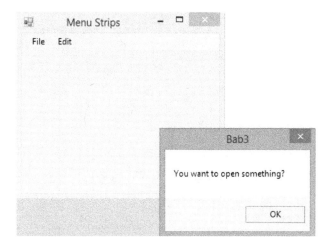

Figure 3.38 Message box that

3.4 Checkboxes

The checkbox is a box that can be checked to choose it. If there are more than one checkboxes in an object (eg: group box), you can choose more than one checkbox.

1. Enter new form item and give it a name FormCheckbox.vb.

Figure 3.39 Inserting new form item for demonstrating checkbox

2. Change the text of the form.

Figure 3.40 Change the text of the form

3. Insert checkbox object on **Common Controls > Checkbox** on the Toolbox panel.

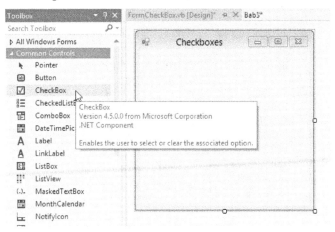

Figure 3.41 Insert checkbox object

4. Enter a label and enter 3 checkboxes.

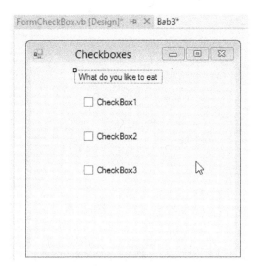

Figure 3.42 Enter three checkboxes

5. Change the text properties for each checkbox and change the name properties, to make the code easier to make.

Figure 3.43 Change name and text

6. Insert a button, change the name and text properties.

Figure 3.44 Insert a button to the form

7. Double-click the button, and enter codes below:

```
        Private Sub btnProses_Click(sender As Object, e As
EventArgs) Handles btnProcess.Click
        Dim foods As String = Nothing
        If Me.cbSatay.Checked = True Then
            foods = Me.cbSatay.Text
        End If
        If Me.cbFriedChicken.Checked = True Then
            foods += ", " + Me.cbFriedChicken.Text
        End If
        If Me.cbKebab.Checked = True Then
            foods += ", " + Me.cbKebab.Text
        End If
        MsgBox(" You like " + foods)

    End Sub
```

Figure 3.45 Entering codes for checkbox

8. Change startup form to existing form.

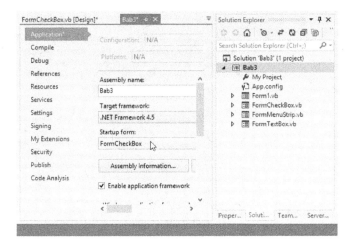

Figure 3.46 Change startup form

9. Run the program by clicking F5.

Figure 3.47 Checkbox program already run

10.   Check items you like, then click **Proses**.

Figure 3.48 Second checkbox is clicked

Figure 3.49 First and third checkbox is selected

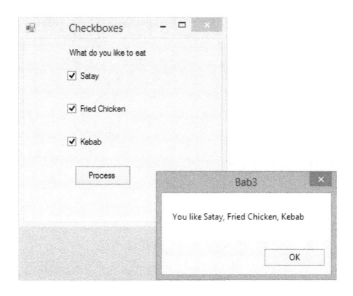

Figure 3.50 All checkboxes selected

3.5 RadioButtons

The radio button is similar with the checkbox, This object can be selected and unselected. If a group of radio buttons placed in a container, like a group box, the radio buttons can only accommodate a single selection.

Some properties of radio buttons are:

- Name: Determine and return Name property from the radio button.

- Checked: Determine and return boolean value from radio button, whether selected or not.

- CanSelect: Determine and return a boolean value, whether radio button can be selected or not.

This is some demonstration on how to use radio button:

1. Insert new item and change the name

Figure 3.51 Insert new form for Radio button demo

2. Change the text properties from the form.

Figure 3.52 Change the text properties from the Form

3. Insert the radio button, by clicking the Radio button in the form.

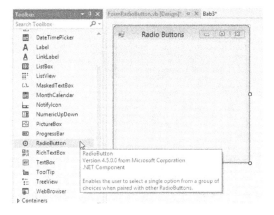

Figure 3.53 Inserting radio button in the form

4. Insert 2 radio buttons, change the text to "Male" and "Female" and change the name with rbMale and rbFemale. Enter one button with text process and name btnProcess

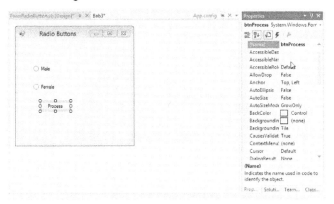

Figure 3.54 Inserting radio button and button

5. Double-click on the button and insert this codes:

```
If Me.rbMale.Checked = True Then
    MsgBox("You are Male")
Else
    MsgBox("You are female")
End If
```

Figure 3.55 Codes to get value from selected radio button

6. Change the startup form to this active form.

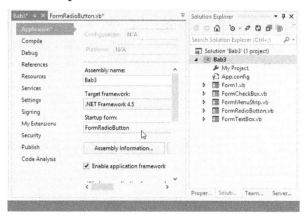

Figure 3.56 Change startup form to this active form

7. Execute the program. When you choose a radio button and click Process button, you'll get a message box depending on the radio button you chose.

Figure 3.57 First radio button clicked and click process

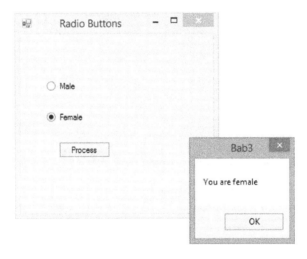

Figure 3.58 Second radio button clicked and click process

3.6 DateTimePickers

Some projects need to do the calculation based on time and date. Visual basic use DateTimePicker object to insert and display a date or time value. This object has some important properties:

- Name: Determine and return name value from the DateTimePicker object.

- MaxDateTime: Determine and return max date and time that can be viewed. The value is read-only

- MinDateTime: Determine and return minimum date and time that can be viewed. The value is read-only.

- MinDate: Determine and return min date that can be chosen

- Value: Determine and return the value of date/time

Here's tutorial to demonstrate the use of the DateTimePicker object in a program:

1. Insert new form in the existing project **Chapter 3** to demonstrate DateTimePicker.

Figure 3.59 Inserting new form for DateTimePicker object

2. Change the text caption of the form.

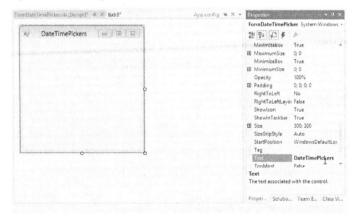

Figure 3.60 Changing the text property, to change text caption

2. After new form inserted, double click on DateTimePicker icon on Toolbox panel to insert DateTimePicker object.

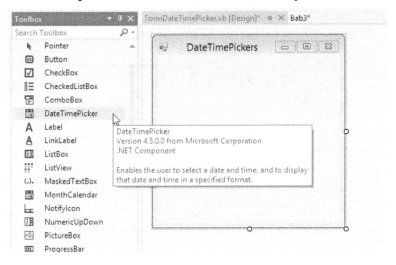

Figure 3.61 DateTimePicker

3. A new DateTimePicker object will emerge on the form.

Figure 3.62 A new DateTimePicker object on the form

4. Double click on DateTimePicker, you can enter codes below:

```
        MsgBox("The date you choose: " +
Me.DateTimePicker1.Value.Day.ToString + " month" +
Me.DateTimePicker1.Value.Date.Month.ToString + " year" +
Me.DateTimePicker1.Value.Date.Year.ToString)
```

Figure 3.63 Codes entered when using Date Time Picker

5. Change the Startup Form of the project to active form that holds DateTimePicker object. Then run the program.

Figure 3.64 Change startup form of the project to activeForm

6. The program will run.

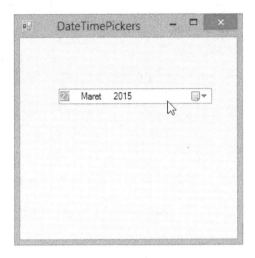

Figure 3.65 The program will run

7. There's a DateTimePicker object on the form. Click the object, a calendar will emerge. Choose a date.

Figure 3.66 Calendar emerge

8. Choose a date you choose. A message box will appear with information about the date you choose.

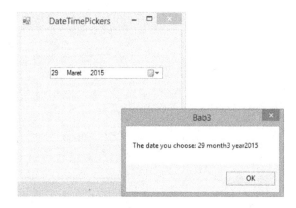

Figure 3.67 Messagebox displaying date chosen

9. You can also click the month and choose a certain month to or years.

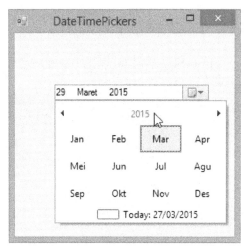

Figure 3.68 DateTimePicker on calendar mode

3.7 Timers and Progress Bars

Timer object involved in a form if you need to create a program that deals with periodical time. A timer don't display interface on the form, it works in the background.

Some properties of the timer object are:

- Name: Determine and return the name of a timer object.

- Enable: Determine and return a boolean value whether this object is enabled or not.

- Interval: Determine and return interval of the timer where something will be executed periodically.

ProgressBar can be used to show the progress of a process. ProgressBar usually used to show progress as an illustration. Some important properties of this object:

- Name: Determine and return the name property of ProgressBar Object.

- Minimum: Determine min value from progress bar.

- Maximum: Determine max value from progressBar.

- Step: Determine interval if function PerformStep() called.

- Value: Determine and return the position of the progress bar.

Here's tutorial on how to program a progress bar:

1. Create a new form for this tutorial. Choose **Windows Form** and give it a name. Click Add button to add this form.

Figure 3.69 Add new form

2. After the form inserted, change the text property for the form.

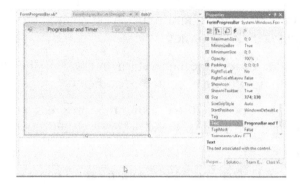

Figure 3.70 Changing the text property of the form

3. Double click progress bar icon on the Toolbox panel. This will insert a ProgressBar object to the form.

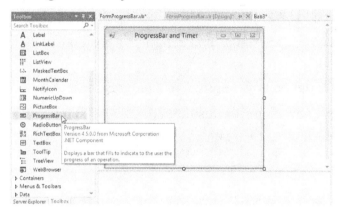

Figure 3.71 Duble click on progress bar

4. A ProgressBar will emerge in the form. You can change the name property of this object.

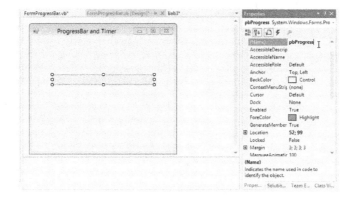

Figure 3.72 New progress bar emerge

5. Double click on Components > Timer on Toolbox panel to insert Timer object. If a timer already inserted, an object with name = Timer1 will emerge.

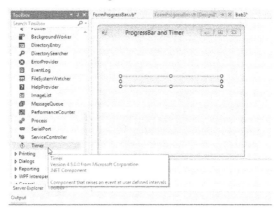

Figure 3.73 Objects Progress Bar and Timer already inserted

6. Set **Enabled** property of the Timer to True. This will make Timer object activated by default without having to write codes.

Figure 3.74 Activate the Timer by setting Enabled to True

7. Double click on timer object. It will automatically create event Timer1_Tick. Insert codes below:

```
Me.pbProgress.Value += 2
If Me.pbProgress.Value <= 30 Then
    Me.Text = "Application Initialized"
ElseIf Me.pbProgress.Value <= 50 Then
    Me.Text = "Application in the the mid of process"
ElseIf Me.pbProgress.Value <= 75 Then
    Me.Text = "Application almost end"
ElseIf Me.pbProgress.Value <= 100 Then
    Me.Text = "Please wait, process completed"
    If Me.pbProgress.Value = 100 Then
        Me.Timer1.Dispose()
    End If
End If
```

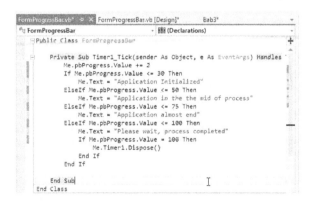

Figure 3.75 Codes for progress bar using timer

8. Right click on the project, choose **Properties** menu and set the Startup Form of the project to this active form.

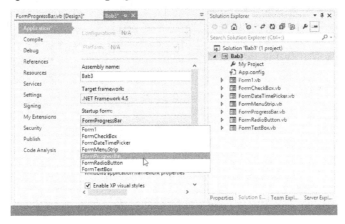

Figure 3.76 Set Startup form to active form Progress bar

9. Run the program.

10. The Titlebar of the application will be dynamically changed because of the Me.Text clause in the codes.

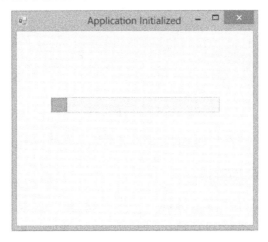

Figure 3.77 Title bar and progress bar at the beginning

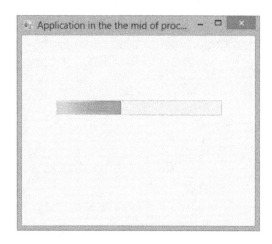

Figure 3.78 Title bar and progress bar in the middle of execution

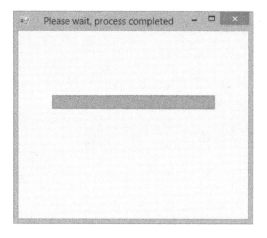

Figure 3.79 Title bar and progress bar after the process completed

3.8 RichTextBoxs

RichTextBox object can open, save, and display RichTextFormat. RichTextBox is an important object if your application handles rich text format. Some important properties of this object:

- Name: Determine and return name value of the RichTextBox object.

- Text: Determine and return values in RichTextBox. The text you can get is the text without formatting.

- RTF: Determine and return object value in RichTextBox, including the formattings.

- Scrollbars: Determine and return scrollbar type in RichTextBox.

- SelectedText: Determine and return selected text value. This text can be formatted using FontStyle from Visual basic.

Here's a demonstration on how to use RichTextBox in a program:

1. Create a new form to do this tutorial. Choose Windows Form type.

Figure 3.80 Choose Windows Form type

2. Change the text property of the form.

Figure 3.81 Changing text property of the form

3. Double click on **Common Controls > RichTextBox** in the Toolbox panel to insert RichTextBox

Figure 3.82 Common Controls > Rich Text Box

4. A RichTextBox object will be inserted on the form.

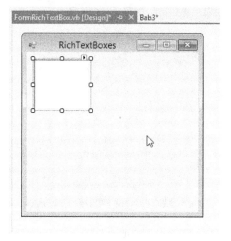

Figure 3.83 RichTextBox inserted

5. Expand the RichTextBox position on the form.

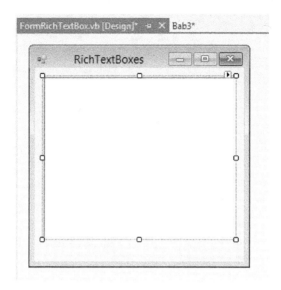

Figure 3.84 Expanding RichTextBox position on the form

6. Change the name property from rich text box object to rtbText.

Figure 3.85 Change name property of RichTextBox object

7. Enter a button and change the text property to "Get text"

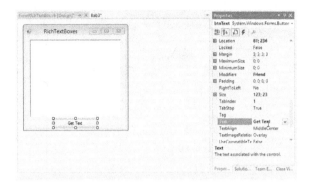

Figure 3.86 Insert a button to get text

8. Change the Name property from the button to btnText to make the codes easier to read.

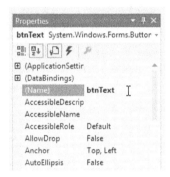

Figure 3.87 Name property

9. Double click on the button.

10. Enter the code to handle btnText_Click like this:

```
MsgBox(Me.rtbText.Text, MsgBoxStyle.Information,
"RTF content without Formatting")
```

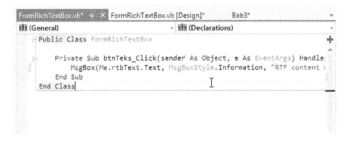

Figure 3.88 Codes to get text from rich text box

11. Before you run the program, change the Startup form to this existing form.

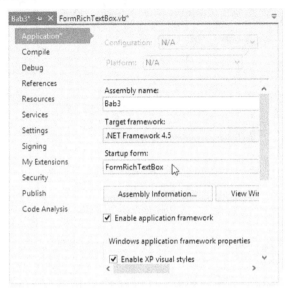

Figure 3.89 Change existing form

12. Run the program, initially richTextbox still empty.

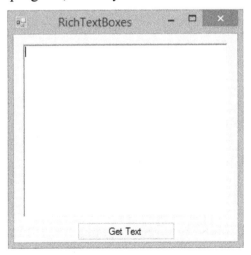

Figure 3.90 RichTextbox still empty at the beginning

13. Enter texts in the rich text box.

14. Click the button.

Figure 3.91 Entering texts to RichTextbox

15. A message box will appear that shows texts inserted to RichTextBox.

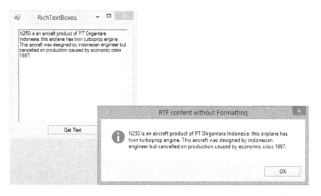

Figure 3.92 Texts from RichTextBox object displayed at message box

3.9 ImageLists and Toolbars

ImageList object can display and save lots of images and saves them in an array. With ImageList, you can save lots of pictures to be used in the program. For example to perform Slideshow in Picturebox, or as an icon on a certain object. Here are some tutorials on how to use ImageLists and Toolbar:

1. Enter new form. Enter the name for this new form in the Name textbox. Click Add.

Figure 3.93 Enter new form

2. Change the new form's text property to "Image List and Toolbar"

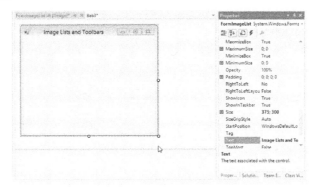

Figure 3.94 Image List and Toolbar

3. Double click on ImageList icon on the Toolbox panel. This will insert ImageList object to the form. If an image list object inserted, below the form will emerge new icon ImageList1.

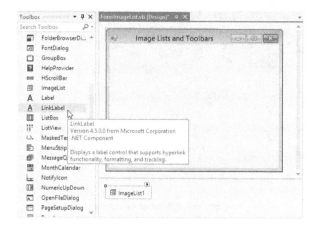

Figure 3.95 ImageList1 will emerge

4. After ImageList inserted, below the form will appear ImageList1 icon. Change the name property if needed.

Figure 3.96 An imageList object already inserted

5. Click on the button [....] in the **Images (Collection)** property.

Figure 3.97 Click on the [...] button

6. An **Images Collection Editor** window appear.

7. Click Add to add new images.

Figure 3.98 ImagesCollectionEditor to insert image into ImageList object

8. Insert images into ImageList by clicking Add button, then choose the picture you want to insert.

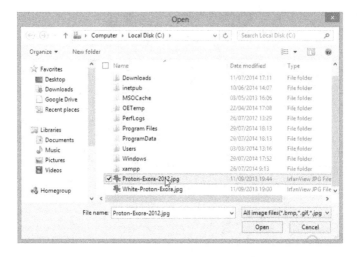

Figure 3.99 Choosing the picture to be inserted into Image List

9. Add images as much as you need it. Click Ok button after that to close this ImagesCollectionEditor window.

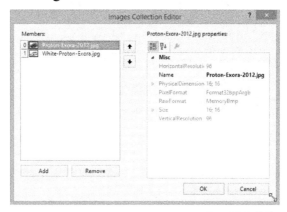

Figure 3.100 Images already inserted

10. Now, enter ToolStrip to create Toolbar. Double click on the ToolStrip object in the Toolbox panel.

11. Above the form, will emerge Image List object.

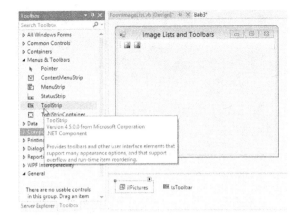

Figure 3.101 Toolstrip object already inserted to create a toolbar

12.   Change the object's property name to tsToolbar.

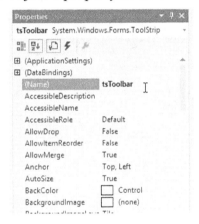

Figure 3.102 Changing the tool strips property name

13. You can insert many objects to the toolbar, the most common objects are buttons. Insert more than one buttons.

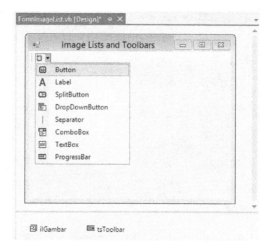

Figure 3.103 Inserting button to Toolstrip

14. Two buttons bill be created, but the icon wasn't available yet. To change the button we'll use codes.

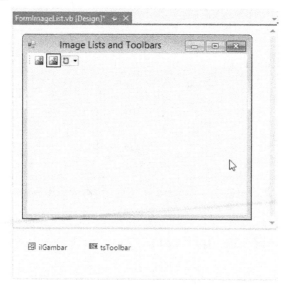

Figure 3.104 Toolbar already created

15. Double-click on the form to insert codes to handle Load event from the form.

```
Me.ToolStripButton1.Image = Me.ilPictures.Images.Item(0)
Me.ToolStripButton2.Image = Me.ilPictures.Images.Item(1)
```

Figure 3.105 Codes to change the image of ToolStripButton image

16. Before running the program, change Startup Form of the project to this active form.

Figure 3.106 Changing startup form to active project

17. Execute the program, the toolbar will have images from the Imagelist.

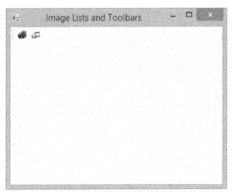

Figure 3.107 Toolbar inserted

133

3.10 Tooltips and ContextMenus

ToolTip and ContextMenu can be accessed if you hover your mouse on a certain part of the projects. Here's an example on how to use ToolTip and ContextMenu in a program:

1. Enter new form into the project.

Figure 3.108 Enter new form to demonstrate ToolTip and ContextMenu

2. Change the text property of the form.

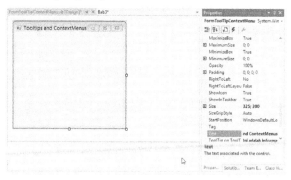

Figure 3.109 Changing the text property

3. Double click on the ToolTip icon in Toolbox, after the tooltip inserted below the form, will emerge ToolTip1 icon. It means the object has already inserted.

Figure 3.110 ToolTip already inserted

4. Change the Name property from tooltip1.

Figure 3.111 Change the name property of Tooltip1 object

5. Double click Menu & Toolbars > ContextMenuStrip to create Context menu. Above the form will appear MenuStrip, and below the form will appear ContextMenuStrip1 icon.

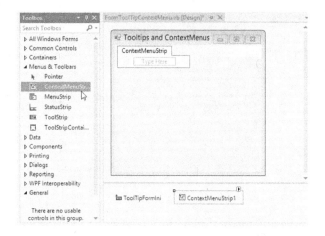

Figure 3.112 Inserting ContextMenuStrip1

6. Change the Name property of the contextMenu.

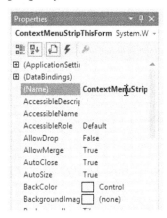

Figure 3.113 Changing the name property of the context menu

7. You can add menu items to ContextMenuStrip by choosing the menu type you want including a separator.

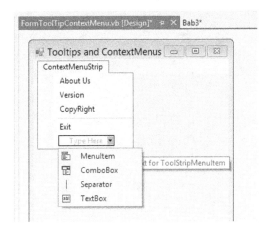

Figure 3.114 Inserting menu item in ContextMenu

8. The menu created will be displayed as a right click menu or context menu.

Figure 3.115 Creating a context menu

9. To attach ContextMenu and Tooltip to object such as Form, first, click the form. Then change the ContextMenuStrip property to the ContextMenuStrip you chose.

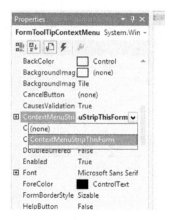

Figure 3.116` Allocate a ContextMenu to a form

10.   Click at the ToolTip object, change the title.

Figure 3.117 Change Tooltip object title

11.   Click Form then look at ToolTip property and set to tooltip
you created before. Enter the texts for the tooltip.

Figure 3.118 Inserting ToolTip content

12.   Change the startup form.

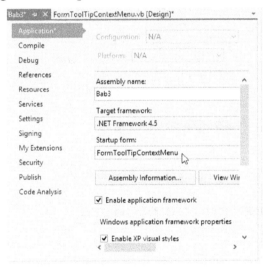

Figure 3.119 Change the startup form

13. When the program run, and you perform a right click on the form. A context menu will appear.

Figure 3.120 ContextMenu

14.   If you hover your mouse on the form, a tooltip will emerge, the title and the text of the tooltip will be the same with the information you entered.

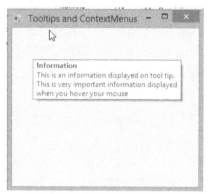

Figure 3.121 a Tooltip displayed

3.11 ListBoxs and ComboBoxs

Listbox and Combobox have a similar function, to show items which user can choose. The ListBox and ComboBox properties also similar. Some of its important properties are:

- Name: Determine and return ListBox object's name.

- SelectedItem: return the selected item.

- Selected Text: Similar with selectedItem, returns selected text.

- Selected Index: Similar with selected item, but only display the integer value of the index. Index starts from 0, the top of the items.

Here's a demonstration on ListBox and ComboBox.

1. Create a new form on this project, insert the Name, and click **Add** to add it.

Figure 3.122 Create new item Windows Form

2. Change form's text property to "ListBox And ComboBox"

Figure 3.123 Change Form's text property

3. Double click ListBox on Toolbox panel to insert ListBox item to the form. A list box item will be inserted

---

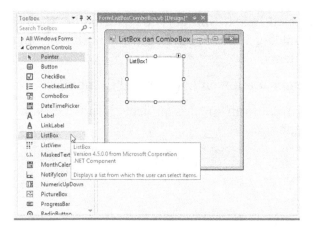

Figure 3.124 ListBox1 inserted

4. Double click on ComboBox to insert combo box.

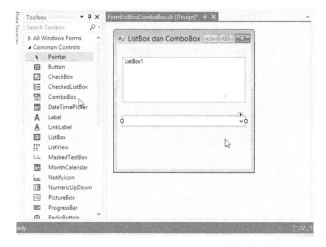

Figure 3.125 Inserting ComboBox

5. To insert an item in Listbox, click on Listbox object, and click Ellipsis button on the right of **Items (Collection)** property.

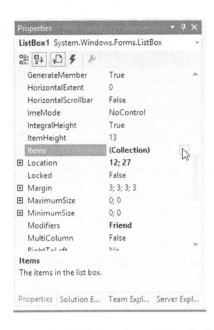

Figure 3.126 Click on Items (Collection)

6. Insert texts in **String Collection Editor**, each line is one item in ListBox. Click **OK** to enter.

Figure 3.127 Inserting items in String Collection Editor

7. You can see list box's content updated.

Figure 3.128 Listbox's content updated

8. With the same method, you can edit the ComboBox's content.

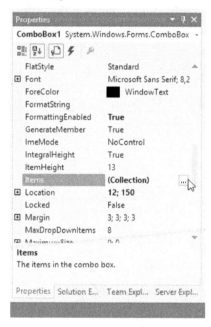

Figure 3.129 Click on Items Property to insert combo box's items

9. Insert some items in combo box. One line is one item. Click OK to insert combo box's items.

Figure 3.130 Inserting items

10. Insert text property for combo box. This text will be displayed by default when combi box hasn't been chosen.

11.   Listbox and Combobox will be updated.

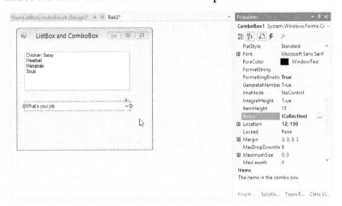

Figure 3.131 Inserting text

12.   Add a button, and change the text property to **Process.**

Figure 3.132 Inserting a button to the form

13.   Change the name property of the button, and double click on the button. Insert codes below:

```
Private Sub btnProses_Click(ByVal sender As System.Object,
ByVal e As System.EventArgs) Handles btnProses.Click
    MsgBox("You like to eat " +
Me.ListBox1.SelectedItem.ToString + " Your hobby is " +
Me.ComboBox1.SelectedItem.ToString, MsgBoxStyle.Information, "
Listbox and Combobox")
    End Sub
```

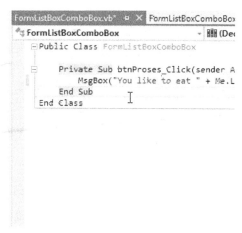

Figure 3.133 Codes to insert

14.   Change startup form to the active form.

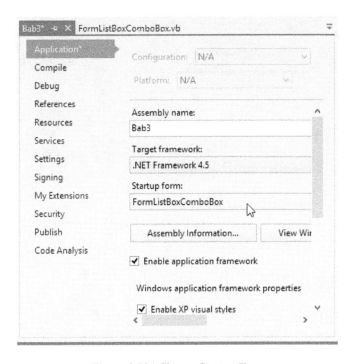

Figure 3.134 Change Startup Form

15.   Run the program.

Figure 3.135 The program runs

16. Choose items in Listbox and Combobox. Then click process.

Figure 3.136 Items chose displayed on message box

3.12 StatusBars

StatusStrip is an object used to make StatusBar. You can use status bar to display information about users, or other information about the program.

There are several important properties of the StatusBar:

- Name: Determine and return statusStrip object's name.

- Background Image: Determine and return the backgrund color of the StatusStrip object.

- Dock: Determine and return docking value of the StatusStrip object.

- CanSelect: Determine and return Boolean value whether MenuStrip can be selectcd by the user or not.

Here's a demonstration on how to use statusBar in a program:

1. Insert new form to the existing project.

Figure 3.137 Insert new form to existing object

2. Change form's text property.

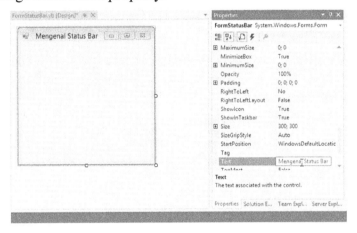

Figure 3.138 Change form's text property

3. Double click on the status strip, on the below of the form, will emerge a StatusStrip object, and below the statusStrip object, there will be an icon StatusStrip1.

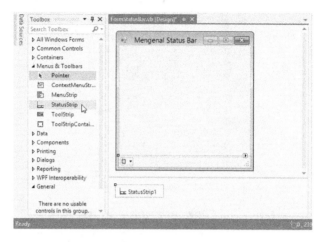

Figure 3.139 StatusStrip inserted to the form

4. You can add many objects to this StatusStrip.

5. Click on the arrow icon, then choose an object, you can choose a StatusLabel, a ProgressBar, a DropDownButton, and a SplitButton.

Figure 3.140 Inserting StatusLabel

6. For StatusLabel, you can change the text property with new texts you like.

Figure 3.141 Entering status property

7. You can customize the status bar with anything you like. Then set this form as Startup form.

Figure 3.142 Add the form as Startup form

8. Then run the program. you'll see the status bar on the bottom of the form.

Figure 3.143 Program with status bar on the bottom

***

ABOUT THE AUTHOR

Ali Akbar is a Visual Basic.NET Author who has more than 10 years of experience in the architecture and has been using Visual Basic.NET for more than 15 years. He has worked on design projects ranging from department store to transportation systems to the Semarang project. He is the all–time bestselling Visual Basic.NET author and was cited as favorite programming author. Zico P. Putra is a senior engineering technician, IT consultant, author, & trainer with 10 years of experience in several design fields. He continues his Ph.D. in the Queen Mary University of London. Find out more at https://www.amazon.com/Zico-Pratama-Putra/e/B06XDRTM1G/

CAN I ASK A FAVOUR?

If you enjoyed this book, found it useful or otherwise then I would really appreciate it if you would post a short review on Amazon. I do read all the reviews personally so that I can continually write what people are wanting.

If you would like to leave a review, then please visit the link below:

https://www.amazon.com/dp/B06XS99PKP

Thanks for your support!

www.ingramcontent.com/pod-product-compliance
Lightning Source LLC
LaVergne TN
LVHW022320060326
832902LV00020B/3572